Comfort
FOR
Your Soul

ARTWORK BY

Carol Endres

HARVEST HOUSE PUBLISHERS

EUGENE, OREGON

Comfort for Your Soul

ISBN 0-7369-0775-0

Design and Production by Garborg Design Works, Minneapolis, Minnesota

Printed in Hong Kong.

03 04 05 06 07 08 09 10 11 / NG / 10 9 8 7 6 5 4 3 2 1

He tends his flock like a shepherd: He gathers the lambs in
his arms and carries them close to his heart.

THE BOOK OF ISAIAH

God beholds thee individually, whoever thou art. "He calls thee by thy name." He sees thee, and understands thee. He knows what is in thee, all thy own peculiar feelings and thoughts, thy dispositions and likings, thy strength and thy weakness. He views thee in thy day of rejoicing and thy day of sorrow. He sympathizes in thy hopes and in thy temptations; He interests Himself in all thy anxieties and thy remembrances, in all the risings and fallings of thy spirit. He compasses thee round, and bears thee in His arms; He takes thee up and sets thee down. Thou dost not love thyself better than He loves thee.

JOHN H. NEWMAN

God, who the universe doth hold
  In His fold,
Is my shepherd kind and heedful,
Is my shepherd, and doth keep
  Me, His sheep,
Still supplied with all things needful.

Francis Davison

5

*I*t was faith in God and His Word that brought Noah and his family on board the ark to be carried through to safety, well-preserved.

A number of years ago, I put my faith in God and His Word to me and stepped on board with Jesus, who has carried me through life blessed and well-preserved.

I thank Him and praise Him for leaving the ninety-nine to find me.

CAROL ENDRES

6

When I look like this into the blue sky, it seems so deep, so peaceful, so full of a

mysterious tenderness, that I could lie for centuries and wait for the dawning of

the face of God out of the awful loving-kindness.

GEORGE MACDONALD

GRANT US THY PEACE, DOWN FROM THY PRESENCE FALLING,

AS ON THE THIRSTY EARTH COOL NIGHT-DEWS SWEET;

GRANT US THY PEACE, TO THY PURE PATHS RECALLING,

FROM DEVIOUS WAYS, OUR WORN AND WANDERING FEET.

ELIZA SCUDDER

7

That He who cares
for the lily,

And heeds the
sparrows' fall,

Shall tenderly lead
His loving child:

For He made and
loveth all.

AUTHOR UNKNOWN

Oh for a closer
walk with God,

A calm and
heavenly frame;

A light to shine
upon the road

That leads me
to the Lamb!

WILLIAM COWPER

Put together all the tenderest love
you know of, the deepest you have
ever felt, and the strongest that has
ever been poured out upon you, and
heap upon it all the love of all the
loving human hearts in the world,
and then multiply it by infinity,
and you will begin, perhaps,
to have some faint glimpse of
what the love of God is.

HANNAH WHITALL SMITH

God's mark of approval, whenever you obey Him, is peace.
He sends an immeasurable, deep peace; not a natural
peace, "as the world gives," but the peace of Jesus.
Whenever peace does not come, wait until it does.

OSWALD CHAMBERS

There may be a promise in the Word which would exactly fit your case, but you may not know of it, and therefore miss its comfort.

CHARLES SPURGEON

THE VALUE OF COMPASSION CANNOT BE OVER-EMPHASIZED... IT TAKES A TRUE BELIEVER TO BE COMPASSIONATE.

ARTHUR H. STAINBACK

God stirs up our comfortable nests, and pushes us over the edge of them, and we are forced to use our wings to save ourselves from fatal falling. Read your trials in this light, and see if your wings are being developed.

HANNAH WHITALL SMITH

God, who gives us His peace, extends rest to the weary and renewal to the exhausted. He wants our souls to be at peace, and He promises to accomplish that peace.

ELIZABETH GEORGE

Oh, the comfort, the inexpressible comfort of feeling safe with a person, having neither to weigh thoughts nor measure words, but pouring them all right out, just as they are, chaff and grain together . . .

DINAH MULOCK CRAIK

"BETWEEN THE HEDGEROWS
OF BORDERS DEFINED,
THE LAND IS SEPARATED
BUT THE HEARTS ENTWINED"

Every heart that has beat strongly and behind it in the world, and bettered

The Lord my pasture shall prepare,
And feed me with a shepherd's care;
His presence shall my wants supply,
And guard me with a watchful eye.

JOSEPH ADDISON

cheerfully has left a hopeful impulse
the tradition of mankind. ROBERT LOUIS STEVENSON

There is a comfort in the strength of love;
'Twill make a thing endurable, which else
Would overset the brain, or break the heart...

WILLIAM WORDSWORTH

He leadeth me, O blessed thought,
O words with heavenly comfort fraught,
Whate'er I do, where'er I be,
Still 'tis God's hand that leadeth me.

JOSEPH HENRY GILMORE

Now God be praised, that to believing souls
Gives light in darkness, comfort in despair!

WILLIAM SHAKESPEARE

Lord, dismiss us with Thy blessing,
Hope, and comfort from above;
Let us each, Thy peace possessing,
Triumph in redeeming love.

ROBERT HAWKER

For this is what the Sovereign LORD says: "I myself will search for my sheep and look after them. As a shepherd looks after his scattered flock when he is with them, so will I look after my sheep. I will rescue them from all the places where they were scattered on a day of clouds and darkness. I will bring them out from the nations and gather them from the countries, and I will bring them into their own land. I will pasture them on the mountains of Israel, in the ravines and in all the settlements in the land…I myself will tend my sheep and have them lie down, declares the Sovereign LORD. I will search for the lost and bring back the strays. I will bind up the injured and strengthen the weak, but the sleek and the strong I will destroy. I will shepherd the flock with justice."

THE BOOK OF EZEKIEL

The very word "God" suggests care, kindness, goodness; and the idea of God in his infinity is infinite care, infinite kindness, infinite goodness. We give God the name of good; it is only by shortening it that it becomes God.

HENRY WARD BEECHER

AN INFINITE GOD CAN GIVE ALL OF HIMSELF TO
EACH OF HIS CHILDREN. HE DOES NOT DISTRIBUTE
HIMSELF THAT EACH MAY HAVE A PART, BUT TO
EACH ONE HE GIVES ALL OF HIMSELF AS FULLY
AS IF THERE WERE NO OTHERS.

A.W. TOZER

Behind the dim
unknown,
standeth God
within the shadow,
keeping watch
above His own.

JAMES RUSSELL LOWELL

NOW IT WAS, THAT
CONFINEMENT WAS TRULY
PAINFUL TO ME; MY SOUL WAS
BURSTING FROM ITS PRISON
TO BE NEAR THE
PILLOW OF MY CHILD, TO
COMFORT, TO STRENGTHEN
HER, TO RECEIVE HER LAST
WISHES, AND TEACH HER
SOUL THE WAY TO HEAVEN!

OLIVER GOLDSMITH
THE VICAR OF WAKEFIELD

Live a little; comfort a little

cheer thyself a little.   WILLIAM SHAKESPEARE

ifficulties, the feeling of security and well-being.

H.L. MENCKEN

Do not be anxious about anything,
but in everything, by prayer and
petition, with thanksgiving, present
your requests to God. And the
peace of God, which transcends
all understanding, will guard
your hearts and your minds...

THE BOOK OF PHILIPPIANS

What do you think? If a man owns a hundred sheep, and one of

them wanders away, will he not leave the ninety-nine on the hills and

go to look for the one that wandered off? And if he finds it, I tell you

the truth, he is happier about that one sheep than about the ninety-

nine that did not wander off. In the same way your Father in heaven

is not willing that any of these little ones should be lost.

THE BOOK OF MATTHEW

All things living He doth feed;
His full hand supplies their need:
For His mercies shall endure,
Ever faithful, ever sure.

Let us then with gladsome mind
Praise the Lord, for He is kind:
For His mercies shall endure,
Ever faithful, ever sure.

JOHN MILTON

Savior, like a shepherd lead us,

much we need Thy tender care;

In Thy pleasant pastures feed us,

for our use Thy folds prepare.

Blessed Jesus, blessed Jesus!

Thou hast bought us, Thine we are.

Blessed Jesus, blessed Jesus!

Thou hast bought us, Thine we are.

DOROTHY ANN THRUPP

O Christ, in Thee my soul hath found,
And found in Thee alone,
The peace, the joy I sought so long,
The bliss till now unknown.

I sighed for rest and happiness,
I yearned for them, not Thee;
But while I passed my Saviour by,
His love laid hold on me.

Now none but Christ can satisfy,
None other name for me;
There's love, and life, and lasting joy,
Lord Jesus, found in Thee.

AUTHOR UNKNOWN

Let nothing disturb thee,
Let nothing affright thee,
All things are passing,
God changeth never.

HENRY WADSWORTH
LONGFELLOW

CAROL ENDRES

Who is it that is your shepherd? The Lord! Oh, my friends, what a wonderful announcement! The Lord God of heaven and earth, the Almighty Creator of all things, He who holds the universe in His hand as though it were a very little thing—He is your shepherd, and has charged Himself with the care and keeping of you, as a shepherd is charged with the care and keeping of his sheep. If your hearts could really take in this thought, you would never have a fear or a care again; for with such a shepherd, how could it be possible for you ever to want any good thing?

HANNAH WHITALL SMITH

The LORD is my shepherd, I shall not be in want. He makes me lie down in green pastures, he leads me beside quiet waters, he restores my soul. He guides me in paths of righteousness for his name's sake. Even though I walk through the valley of the shadow of death, I will fear no evil, for you are with me; your rod and your staff, they comfort me. You prepare a table before me in the presence of my enemies. You anoint my head with oil; my cup overflows. Surely goodness and love will follow me all the days of my life, and I will dwell in the house of the LORD forever.

THE BOOK OF PSALMS